Kitte

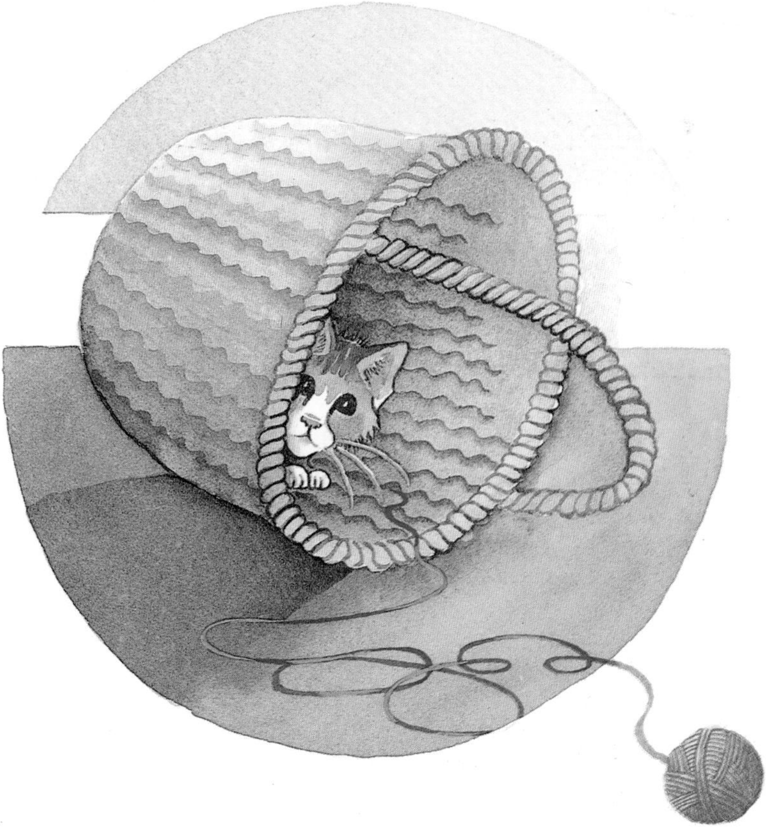

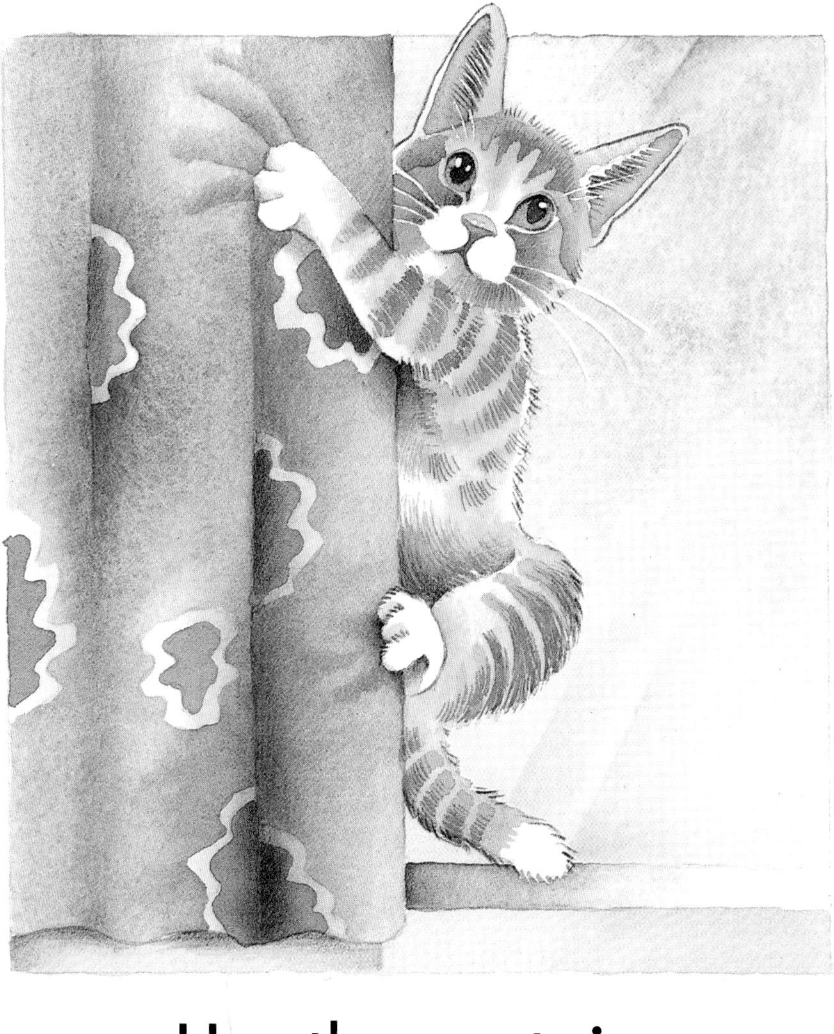

Up the curtain,

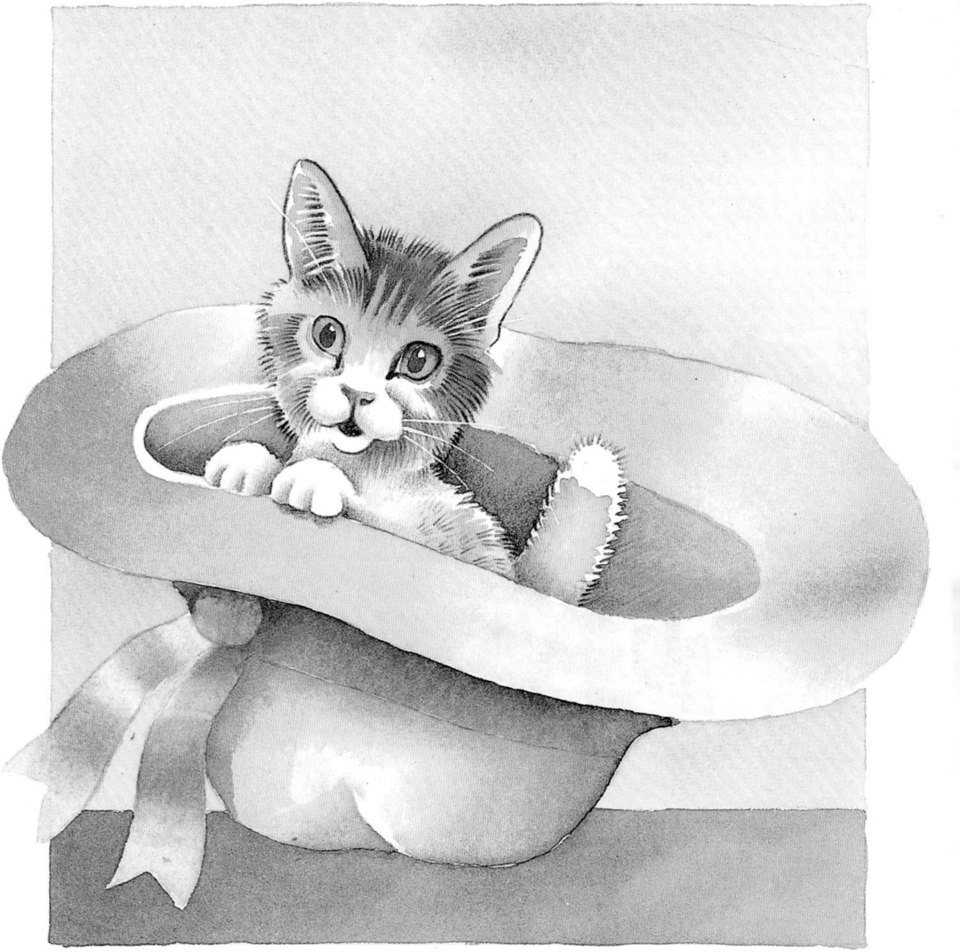

in the hat,

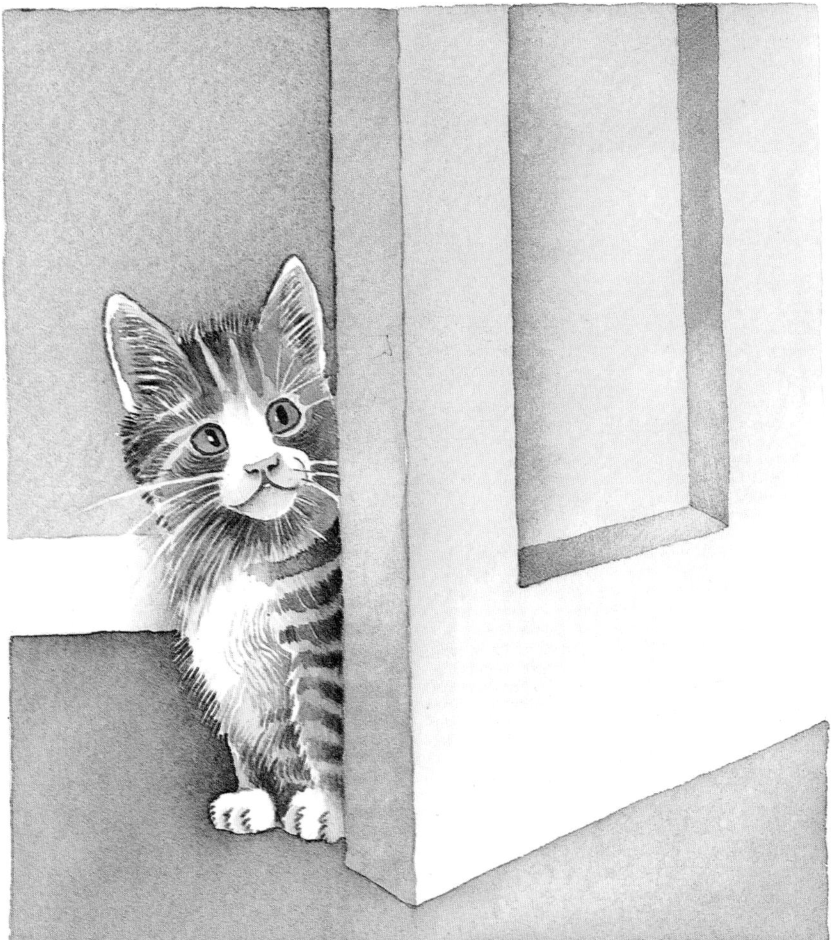

behind the door,

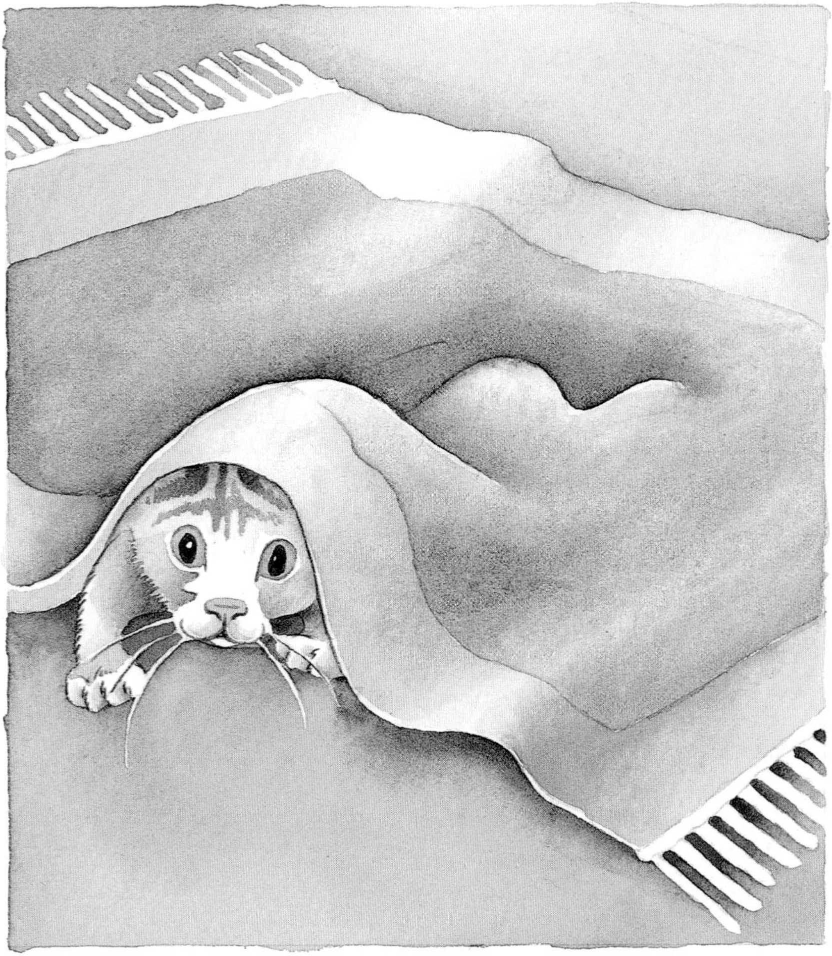

under the mat,

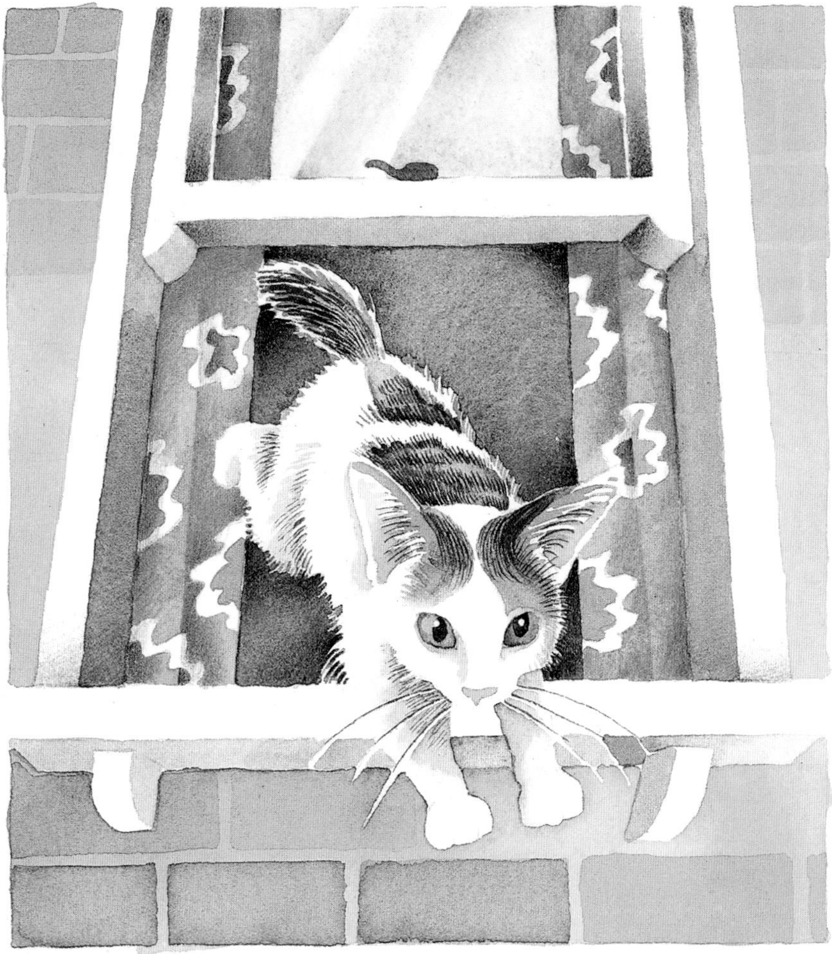

out the window,

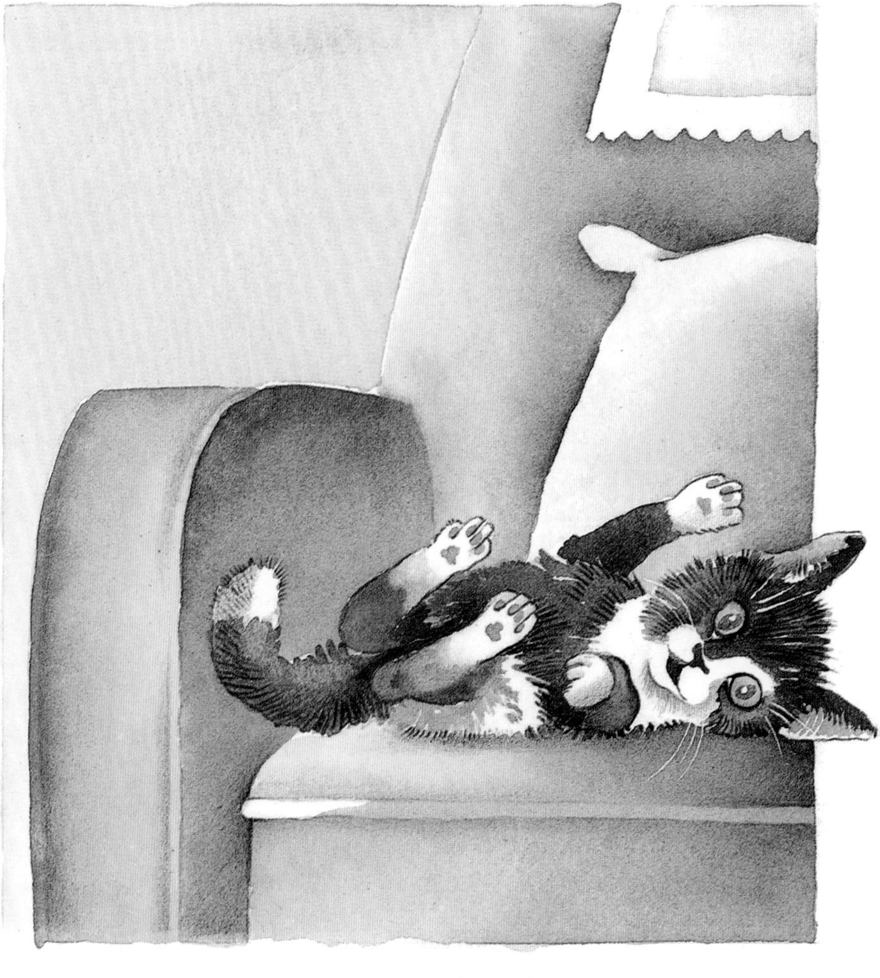

on the chair —

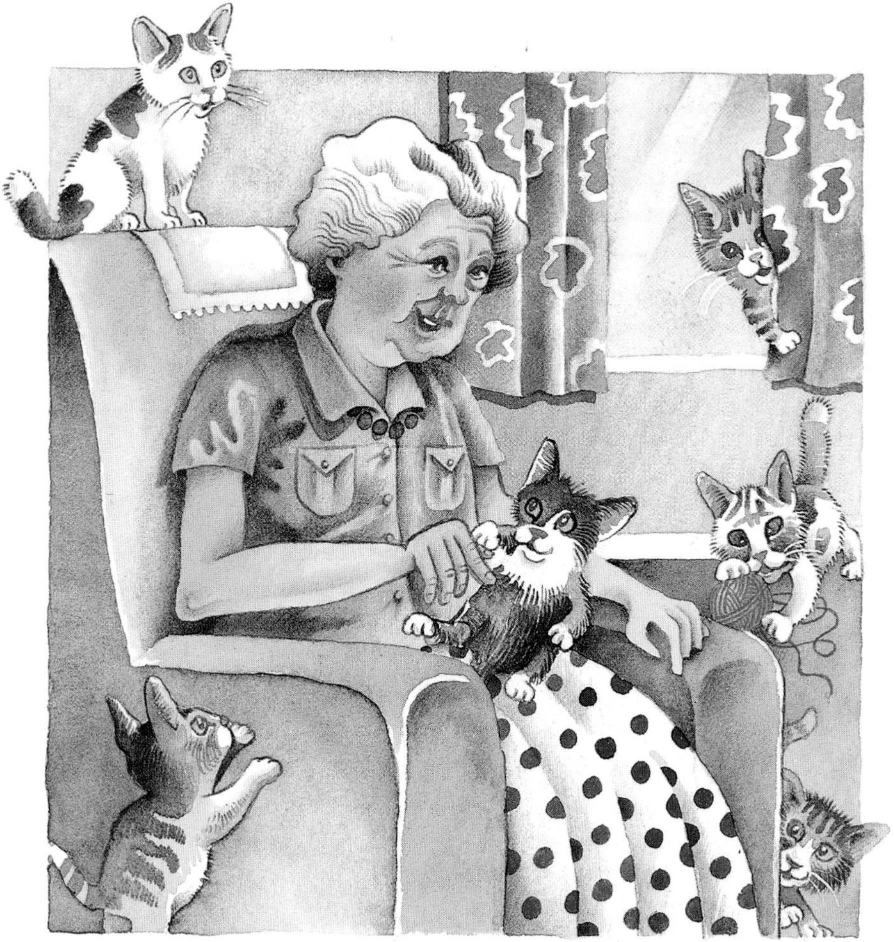

Grandma's kittens
are everywhere.